SO YOU WANT TO KEEP SEAHORSES

By

Tom Hornsby

Introduction

For many years I have thought about writing a book about my passion, seahorses. There are already many other books on the market about these beautiful creatures and I did not want to add another that would be similar.

Then I realised that what was missing, was not a book about seahorses, but rather, a book about how to keep seahorses in the home aquarium, how to raise the fry and how to recognise issues these exotic creatures have in our aquariums.

I have been answering questions regarding these seahorse issues for some years now. So this book is to help new seahorse keepers with the most basic questions and the most complex issues. I hope you find this information useful.

Hippocampus Erectus seahorse bred by the Author

Chapters   page

Chapter 1

The Aquarium

The aquarium is a very important piece of equipment used for housing your pet. There are many types of aquarium for sale today, and no one aquarium is the perfect sort. There are criteria that need to be adhered to for the comfort of your seahorse, and then there is your personal preference as well.

There are quite a few seahorses on the market today, and they grow to various sizes, so if you know which breed of seahorse you want to get then you can work out the tank size you will require for your seahorses. Most people do not know if they want two or four seahorses, but for now we shall think about having four seahorses in our tank. Two males and two females.

The amount of water you need in your tank, to keep seahorses is easy to work out. You will require at least 130 litres of water for the first pair of seahorses, and then another 40 litres of water for the second pair of seahorses. So for four seahorses the minimum water capacity of the tank should be at least 170 litres of water.

Another consideration with seahorses is the tank height. The seahorse, when full grown, will reach a length of beetween 15 and 18 centimeters, depending on the breed you purchase. So your tank should be three times the full grown height of your seahorses. You can see the average size seahorses grow to on page 18, multiply the height by 3 and you can tell the height of the tank that you will require. Seahorses do a unique dance every morning and every night, and need the correct height to accomplish their dance. They also practise this dance for the occasions when they swop eggs, so the height is very important to them.

They are very messey eaters and, due to their rudimentary stomaches and their continual eating, they also defecate a lot more than most marine fish. For this reason the tank should be easily accessible for cleaning. Remember a 3 foot deep tank is beautiful to look at but you would have to have amazingly long arms to reach the bottom of it for cleaning, and reaching things that you wish to adjust. There are some different types of tanks on the market and these are explained below.

1   Tanks with overhead filtration, Aqua one T620 is 130 litres and can house 2 seahorses

2   Reef tanks with sumps, excellent choice see AquaReef 195 as example, housing 4 seahorses

3   Plug and play reef tank,   Aquamedic 270 litre kauderni holds 6 seahorses comfortably

4   Tanks with external filter …. Can be any make as long as the tank is higher than 20 inches and the litres are over 180. There are a few good makes of external filters, Fluval, Eheim, and Aqua One being some examples

5   Tanks made to your own specification

Once you have decided on a suitable size tank for your seahorses, you will have to think about the equipment you will need to run it. There are many opinions about what is right and what is wrong, but these are the various things you will need, and an explanation of what they do and how they do it.

The skimmer

This is a pump that creates bubbles in a chamber, which are then channeled into a funnel, where they are collected at the top in a cup. You will need to empty the cup regularly and the smell is really bad. This is because all the tiny waste particles are caught up in the bubbles and deposited in the cup of the skimmer. If you have a stand alone tank the skimmer can hang on the back of the tank, or some can stand in the tank. If you do not want to purchase a skimmer then you can do larger more frequent water changes, and reduce the tiny waste particles this way. At this point I would like to mention that an external filtration unit such as a Fluval or Eheim will also help to keep the waste down in a stand alone tank. This takes the water out of the tank, passes it through a series of sponges and different substrats and then through filter floss, before returning the water to the tank.

The heater

The heater, if it is in the tank with the seahorses, needs a protective cover to stop the seahorses burning their tails on it, when they hitch onto it. The heat for most tropical seahorses is around 71F to 74F. Too hot will cause bacteria to multiply, out of control, and this will cause an oxygen depletion in the tank, which in turn will lead to the seahorses breaking out in stress related illnesses, often killing them.

Water movement

You have to move the water around in a marine tank to avoid stagnation in the corners and in other dead spots (areas where the water is not being moved) and again there are many ways of doing this. The first is by adding power head pumps to the tank that suck in the water and blow it out, moving the water in it's path around. The second is using wave makers, pumps that pulsate and move the water around. The third, if you do not have a sump, the next best thing, is to use an external filter box. This sits on the floor behind the tank, and contains some filter substrat, and some sponges and has spaces for you to add your own medium to help your tank have good quality water. The water is taken out to the external box by gravity and is returned by a small pump in the box. The returned water comes in through a funnel or through a spray bar. To have a gentle flow in your tank particularly for the smaller seahorses you can use an additional pump that attaches to a spray bar. The spray bar sprays the water over the surface of the aquarium, and moves the water more gently so smaller seahorses can manage to swim in the current. The effect of spraying water over the top of the tank water is also to oxygenate the tank water more.

Power heads and wave makers

Power heads are pumps that take in the water and then pump it out into the tank creating water movement. The amount of movement is measured in Litres per Hour (LPH). So if you want a powerful movement, say 1200 LPH, then you would look at the LPH on the pump first. The way the water is spurted out is also varied. Like a garden hose attachment that lets you jet wash spray or mist the plants, these pumps can also send out different spray patterns. Seahorses do not cope well in a powerful spray that moves them across the tank at speed, as they are poor swimmers.

But many keepers report that their seahorses like the more gentle flow and are seen to constantly

return to the power head to 'go with the flow' or to ride the current across the tank. It does take

a little trial and error to get the flow correct, but the most important thing is to avoid the seahorse

being able to hitch on the powerhead and get it's tail anywhere near the fan blades. These will

damage the tail of the seahorse and will cause a most terrible injury to the tail, leading to it's

death.

Wavemakers are pulsating powerheads that can be controlled to make gentle or strong water

movement, and many keepers buy these with electronic controls allowing them to be set at

higher flow in daytime, lower flow at night, with great success.

The sump

You may also be able to get a tank with a separate sump under the tank, where the water from

the tank is dropped to the sump and is pumped from the sump back into the tank, once it has

gone through a cleaning process. Here you can put your skimmer and your heater and a few

more useful things, along with a return pump which will pass the processed water back to the

aquarium.

If you have the separate sump you can add some macro algae called cheto which will eat the

phosphate, bringing the phosphate levels down. Phosphates are the waste from fish corals and

food. A small light source over the cheato, 24/7, helps to keep the cheato growing and using

the phosphates day and night for food. You may wonder what phosphates are, well they are the

waste from the tank, and they use the nitrates from the tank cycle, and they are consumed by the macro algae, so high phosphates gives you hair algae which is unsightly, and cheato uses the nitrates and phosphates to grow, and thereby reduces the nusciance algae in the tank. You can read more about phosphates when you read about the water cycle.

Filtration

You need to have some sort of filtration in your tank, and here the choices are endless. You can add live rock and live sand, or even man made rock and dry sand, (the benefits being no hitch hikers in dry sand and man made rock to hurt the seahorses). You can add macro algae to the tank, and it will grow in the sand or on the rock and provide hitches for the seahorses and form an important part of your tank filtration. Basically all the filtration helps hold and colonise the bacteria, and the bacteria processes the fish waste for you. You can add clean up crew to help control the waste matter also. There are products to put in the sump or external filter box that help bacteria to grow by using a micro-pore structure which provides a high surface area, for the bacteria engaging in the decomposition of toxins, generated as part of the nitrogen cycle. The better the substrate, the more stable the water in the tank. So you would be better to buy a good quality product.

Water cycle and parameters

The water you add to the tank for the seahorses should be 1.022 to 1.024 salinity, temperature also around 22 degrees centigrade to 24 degrees centigrade. The water has to do a cycle before you can add anything live to it. This means that it has to have some ammonia in the water to start the cycle off. If you have a second tank already, you can use some of the waste water from a water change. If this is your first tank you will have to add something to start producing the ammonia. Once the live rock is in the tank, and some live sand, the ammonia will start to come from the bacterae in the live rock and sand. If you are not using live rock and live sand you can add ammonia and test the water to see how quickly it converts it to nitrites, and then to nitrates. With live rock and live sand wait 2 weeks then perform a water change of 20 percent, wait another 2 weeks and do another water change of 20 percent, then after the first 6 weeks test your water. If it is holding the nitrites and ammonia at zero and the nitrates have also gone down to around 10 then you are almost there. You could add some clean up crew next and then a few weeks later a fish or two, and after 12 weeks if all the ammonia and nitrite readings are good and the nitrates are very low, you can add the seahorses.

The next page has a photo of my 350 Litre tank with hang on the back skimmer and an external filtration box. The other filtration in this tank is the live rock, sand, caulerpa and other macro algaes. This is a Jewel Trigon 350 and has blue backing on the glass to the left of the tank. I clean this tank by using a magnetic glass cleaner every morning on the viewing screens. I remove any dead or dying algae as I see it. I empty the skimmer cup every three days as a rule. I change the water, aproximately 50 litres, once a week and remove some every day when I remove the uneaten food. The external filter needs separate maintenance every 12 weeks, changing the filter wool and rinsing the sponges in the waste water from the water change. I change the filter floss in the Jewel Chamber as required, which is normally weekly, and then I can sit back and enjoy the seahorses.

Setting the aquarium up

So once you have decided on the tank you want and the set up you are going to use for it (filtration and equipment), you need to position it, in your room. Make sure that it is not near a window where the sun will shine on it, as this will make the temperature unstable. Put the tank somewhere where the traffic in the room is not heavy, so the fish are not stressed.

Make sure your floor is strong and level, the tank will be heavy when full of rocks, sand and water. Before you place your tank in it's final position, if you want to put backing material onto the glass at the back of the tank, now is the time to do it. Do not push your tank right back to the wall as you may need to reach behind it from time to time. Make sure the power source is at least a safe distance from the water and the water splashes you will make when attending to the tank. Then sort out the external filters or sump, and get the equipment in place. Add all the water and then place the rocks in the tank, making sure they are firm and will not topple over onto your seahorses or against the tank, breaking the glass. If you are using coral sand, add it now and you will not see inside the tank again for a few hours as it will be all murky. Once you have the filtration and the pumps in place power up, and wait.

You will have to be patience as this can take some time, waiting for the debris to settle, but once it has, this is the time to check the flow for dead spots and the rocks for stability. Wait for the tank to cycle. This is the most frustrating wait of all, as you must wait until the tank cycles properly before you add anything to your tank. You should have a test kit available, although your local fish shop may provide a water testing service for you. Either take a sample of water to the fish shop, at least 100 ml, so they can perform the tests, or test it yourself at home.

The water has to do a cycle before you can add anything live to it. Read the cycling methods and process earlier in this book on page 10.

The cycle happens like this. The ammonia builds up and the ammonia test will show very positive, then gradually the ammonia will go down and the nitrites will show very positive. After a while the nitrites will go down and the nitrates will go up, still not good for adding anything to the tank except perhaps, the rivershrimp. Eventually the nitrates will go down and the ammonia and the nitrites will be at zero. The nitrates then go up and after a while they come down, to between 4 and 10, and your tank will have cycled.

Test the ammonia nitrites and nitrates and make a note of it in 2 weeks, then perform a water change of 20 percent, wait another 2 weeks, test and make a note again of the results, and do another water change of 20 percent, then after the first 6 weeks test your water. If it is holding the ammonia and nitrites at zero and the nitrates have also gone down to around 10 then you are almost there. You could add some clean up crew next, and then, a few weeks later a fish or two, and after 12 weeks, if all the readings are good, add the seahorses.

For the clean up crew, add snails first, cerith and nassarius and feed a tiny frozen mysis at night, as now you have to feed the clean up crew. In a couple more weeks you can add a few more clean up crew. Sand sifting stars can be added after a few months once the sand is full of the food they live on. They will die if you get them too soon. Once the tank has cycled and the clean up crew is added, you may like to seed the tank with copepods and other critters that the seahorses can eat. Add some on a weekly basis, and now go about choosing your seahorses. You can add live corals, but only mushrooms, toadstools, gorgonian and non stinging corals.

Gorgonian with Barbouri seahorses in residence

Chapter 2

The Seahorses available to the hobby

Choosing Your Seahorses

Before rushing out to buy your seahorses from the local pet store you need to be aware of a few things. Seahorses can be caught straight from the sea, and therefore are wild caught. These seahorses will need to be checked over for worms, flukes, parasites and abceses. They will not eat frozen food and may never eat frozen food, so be prepared to have to supply live food every day of their lives. This may sound easy, but often in bad weather or rough seas the live food can not be caught.

The treatment they may require to bring them to good health can be extensive, so for that reason consider buying your seahorses from a reputeable seahorse breeder. Then your seahorse will be in good health, will be sexed and will be taking frozen mysis as part of it's staple diet. If you go to a good breeder you will also be advised of the basic conditions the seahorse has been kept in until the time you purchase him. The easiest way to settle a new seahorse into your tank is to match, as near as possible, the conditions of the breeder's tank. The photoperiod, the temperature and the salinity, the brand of food and any enrichments added and how often. All this information makes the transition from the breeder to the new keeper's home far more comfortable for the seahorse. Stress is not good for seahorses so having this matching set up will reduce a lot of the stress caused when you rehome him.

Buying from a breeder

So you need to find a reputable breeder to purchase your seahorse from. If you can make a visit and choose the ones you like, all the better, but many breeders only deliver or post, but you can request a photo first. There are many breeders available in the UK.

Most seahorses purchased from breeders and are truly aquarium bred. These should be parasite free and eating frozen food. They should have a good weight and be a reasonable size for the breed. Ready to go into a normal size tank and to cope with the flow and feeding in the tank. To check that they are healthy and well fed, look at the front of the seahorse and the side of the chest of the seahorse. There you will see the underlying bony structure, and the skin between the segments of the base structure should be full and fleshy.

The photo on the next page is an example of two healthy well fed seahorses. They are two years old and part of my breeding herd.

Hippocampus Erectus

The male is on the right of the photo and the dark patch at the end of the body is his brood pouch full of fry. The female is at the top of the photo and her body meets her tail and there is no brood pouch. In fact her body tucks up slightly to the tail and at the very point of her body and it is there you sometimes see the egg depositor when she is gravid (full of eggs).

Available seahorses in the UK

These are some of the seahorses that can be purchased in the UK and that are tank bred.

Hippocampus Reidi – Brazilian seahorse   grows to 20 cm

Hippocampus Kuda – Spotted seahorse   grows to 14 cm (larger ones to 18cm)

Hippocampus Erectus – Lined seahorse   grows to 19 cm

Hippocampus Whitei – White's seahorse   grows to 8 cm

Hippocampus Comes – Tiger Tail Hippocampus   grows to 18 cm

Hippocampus Barbouri - Barbour's seahorse   grows to 15 cm

Hippocampus Angustus – Narrow Bellied seahorse   grows to 22 cm

Hippocampus Fuscus – Sea Pony   grows to 14 cm

Hippocampus Abdominalis – Pot bellied seahorse   grows to 35 cm

Hippocampus Taeniopterus – Common   grows to 18 cm

Hippocampus Zosterae – Dwarf   grows to 3 cm

When choosing your seahorse you will need to consider how much height you need to have for them in the tank, and how many seahorses you eventually would like in your tank. A basic tank to hold one pair of seahorses should hold 130 Litres of water, and be 3 times the final height of the seahorse you wish to purchase. So for an Hipocampus Erectus you would need 3 times the final height which is around 8 inches. So a tank with water 24 inches deep would be really good for this pair. If you want to add more seahorses you need to buy a tank with 130 litres for the first two seahorses and another 40 litres for each additional pair, so if you want six eventually you would buy a tank 210 litres, (130+40+40 litres). A sumped tank is always of more use with seahorses as you can add more filtration equipment to the sump.

Adding the seahorses to the tank

Before adding the seahorse make sure your water parameters are the same as the parameters the seahorse has been kept in by the shop or breeder, temperature salinity and pH. If there is a big difference add some of your water to the bag to equalise the conditions. This will take a while, half an hour or much more if there is a big difference in salinity. Better to get the tank correct before you collect the seahorses though, so it matches the parameters of the breeder's water. Then you can float the bag for 15 minutes and then 5 minutes to add your water and then release the seahorses. Offer some food to them shortly after their release. They normally eat almost straight away, especially if from a breeder. If you do get them from a fish shop it is important to see them eating frozen mysis, and also to get the salinity and the temperature etc from the shop keeper when you purchase them.

Water should be at 21 to 23 degrees Centigrade, 71 to 74 degrees Fareheit and salinity between 1.021 and 1.024. PH 8.2. I go for the higher salinity but that is personal preference.

Remember Pot Bellied seahorses are kept in temperate water at around temperature 19°C (66°F), pH 8.2, salinity 1.022. These also require a chiller to keep the tank cool enough.

Once you have your seahorses you must be very regular with your tank hygiene and water changes. Any waste will build up on the bottom of the tank and the seahorses often sit on the bottom of the tank looking under rocks for tasty morsels. The toxic waste on the floor can poison the seahorses. So the best way is to remove uneaten food before it can harm them, good clean up crew or manually clean it out with an air line.   At least once a day this should be cleared up along with the large poops they do. These float around and get caught up on the hitches and corals etc. and cause a rise in phosphates, leading to water quality issues and nusiance algae.

Water changes should be done using about 25% of the total tank volume weekly to start with when you first add the seahorses and fortnightly once the tank has stabelised. Check the water for ammonia, nitrites and nitrates on a daily basis, when they are first added to the tank, as they are very sensitive to water quality. Keeping seahorses is all about keeping good water quality and sustained parameters.

Feeding the seahorses

They need feeding on a regular basis, two to three times a day, and I feed all mine (except the dwarfs) on mysis which I enrich regularly with New Era spray on enrichment. My seahorses have this all their lives and live long and healthy lives, breeding on a regular basis.

I use Gamma Mysis as it does not deteriorate as quickly as the non-radiated foods do. This helps keep the water quality good for a longer period, but the waste food still must be cleared up every day. Clean up crew do help clearing up the uneaten food. There are many other Mysis foods available, but if they are not irradiated you should clear the waste after a short while. They eat a variety of live foods as well. Live mysis and small river shrimps are a favourite of Reidi and Erectus. Although Kuda just do not seem interested in the river shrimp, but they do chase the

Bahia mysis all around their tank. Live adult enriched brine shrimp (artemia) is not good for seahorses as the food value in artemia is very low, and they will not gain much from it. I use it for a week when weaning the fry before getting them onto frozen mysis, or when they are refusing to eat, but do not get them to rely on it, as it will not help them to fill out. It would be like feeding a child on sweets, for all the goodness in it. Krill is also a shrimp that seahorses love to eat. Frozen krill that is gamma radiated is a good treat for them.

If you start this way with your adults you will find they grow well for you, with regular feeds and routine water changes and daily tank maintenance.

Adding different seahorses to the same tank

Now you may want to know about mixing seahorses in the same tank, and mixing wild caught seahorses from the sea with seahorses that are aquarium bred. It is not a good idea. Mixing different species can lead to them being exposed to each other's pathogens (bacteria). Mixing wild caught that have all the bacteria that come with being taken from the sea, whether directly or from pens or tanks in the sea where they are raised, with seahorses bred in the aquariums, with no contact with the seas, can cause all sorts of problems . An example is when the ones from the breeders catch worms from the ones from the sea, or the ones from the sea become stressed in an aquarium and become sick and pass this to healthy aquarium bred ones.

Some keepers like to have a collection of different seahorses in their tank, and they add various species, all from different breeders. You may imagine this is OK but I have seen friends, who are expert keepers, loose all of one species when adding another species. I have done it in the past, when I first kept these beautiful creatures, and successfully kept H. Comes with H. Reidi and they all lived together until they died of old age. Then I kept H. Kuda with H. Reidi and the H. Kuda died. I nearly always keep them separate now.

I have one male H. Barbouri with H. Erectus, as the H. Barbouri was the only one of 6 fry I managed to rear. He was only an inch long when I introduce the H. Erectus to keep him company. They became very closely bonded, and he (I thought he was female at the time) and the female have stayed together for almost a year now.

He has all the H. Erectus habits, he eats so well and chases the food, gets into scrums with the others, but is a really beautiful H. Barbouri. I have other H. Barbouri growing up now and hope there is a female in the group, to pair him with eventually. They are the most stunning seahorses and their fry are hitching from birth, and easily fed on newly hatched artimea. They have reasonably large fry compared to H. Reidi which have very small fry.

The photo on page 23 is of two of my beautiful H. Barbouri, and you can see the markings on their snouts which helps to identify these pretty little seahorses. They also have spines on their body that are white at the bottom and the tip and black in the middle, which give a sparkling effect as they swim.

The Barbouri with his female and other pairs in the tank now

The female has just passed some eggs to the male so in this photo she is looking hollow in the lower part of her body.

H. Barbouri have beautiful markings on their snout and are covered in spines which are light with a dark band in the middle which makes them sparkle when they swim.

Chapter 3

Seahorse behaviour in the aquarium

Seahorse dancing and fighting

I often get asked about why the H. Erectus sehorses I have just sold, are fighting. The new keepers are really concerned as the larger one is 'bullying' the smaller one. The male is pulling the female around by her tail and dragging her all over their aquarium. He is changing colour and if they have more males in the tank he is showing aggression toward them. This is normally on the next morning after adding them to their new tank. I aways smile to myself about this, as it is going to happen most mornings for the rest of the seahorse's lives. This is the start of the mating dance.

Some seahorses do mate for life and if one dies the other can die soon after. Many others are very gregarious, and in my tanks where there may be a group of six pairs, one boy may attempt to take eggs from four of the females, in one day. Especially where they are very young and inexperienced. The bright orange eggs are lying on the bottom of the tank and the females are all egg less. Very annoying for me as the eggs are not there when their own partner wants them, and the youngster is still after eggs after the unsuccessful attemps to get them.

The girls get their eggs ready before the male they are paired with, gives birth. At this point the male dances with such passion in the morning and night, and the girl often is near to him in the aquarium all day, while he sits quietly in a place where he can wait for the event. Once the fry are expelled the male will often be pregnant again within hours of giving birth. Jealousy sometimes arises in the tank with the males over a particular female. The males will snick at each other and sometimes at the female, if she accepts the advances of a male other than her mate, but these squabbles soon pass with no long term damage to any seahorse.

Once eggs have been swopped the males become quieter for a few days, only moving around to eat and dance, or for a little exercise now and then. They eat well and grow a very large pouch, and, as the day for the fry to arrive gets nearer, they become more persistent in the dancing with their female. The purpose of this is to get the female ready with the next lot of eggs, so that after the birth he will be able to fill his pouch again. These males live to give birth and propogate the species. I call them the rabbits of the oceans.

The females are far more active than the males and spend days hunting amongst the rocks and sitting together in groups, playing in the flow and watching their males. They are first to come for the food each morning and dance up and down the glass to get our attention. Smaller seahorses introduced to a tank of adults are so inquisitive that they start at the bottom of a large female and swim up to the top where they encircle the female's head two or three times and then stop and have an eye to eye with them. It is so funny to see. The adults tolerate this and the young hanging on to them with good nature.

A large H. Erectus with a pouch full of fry.

When the fry arrive the seahorses do not eat them, although they do watch with interest. Sometimes the one giving birth has another seahorse hitching onto him, very uncomfortable, but they soon separate. Once they have all been born the male spends time flushing his pouch to make it ready for the eggs the female has ready for him. It is always good to make sure you have done a water change a couple of days before the birth, so the seahorse has clean water to flush with, both before and after the birth.

Handling your seahorse

If the seahorse changes from his normal colour to a dark one it is normally a sign that something is wrong. It is not a bad thing to hold the seahorse and check him over. Wash your hands and make sure there is no trace of any chemicals on them, or hand cream or soap. Then grasp the seahorse around the body with your finger and thumb, and without lifting him out of the water examine him for any bumps or colour discolouration and general swellings. Check his gills are not red and that his snout is clear. See that he has a strong tail grasp, as he will be holding on to your spare fingers. You may sense a clicking in his chest, this is him saying 'let go' but, for a few seconds it will not hurt him to be held. Check for a sore tail tip, or a foreign body attached to the seahorse, bristle worm spines, tears in his skin, and any other thing that might be stressing him. Sometimes a small aiptasia can attach to the seahorse, which can be wiped gently away with a cotton wool ball.

If your seahorse is floating or having difficulty manoevering then it will be something more serious. Some male seahorses get gas bubble disease in their pouches, and it can be caused by something in the womb, that should not be there, causing gas to be produced. Do not panic as this can be easily sorted out for the seahorse if you are gentle and patient with them. Do not be afraid to act, as leaving these conditions can lead to death. If one is laying on the floor for some time, and I mean hours, and he has been quiet for a few days, perhaps not eating, then it is time to take hold of him and check him out for issues. So read the last chapter, When your seahorse is ill, and follow the directions there.

Finding your seahorse

Being shy creatures, you will play hunt the seahorse quite regularly, but do try to resist moving

the rocks and the algaes to find them. They do normally surface when you feed them. They can

lay on their side searching out small crustations for hours at a time. Only their eyes will move.

I was looking for one of my black and white erectus one morning and could not see her. Then I looked at the pink plastic plant in the bare bottom breeding tank and she was there, in the pink, so to speak, right in front of me. So they are chameleons and can catch us out. I watched one change to a glorious pale colour for the female he was trying to impress, and 20 seconds later he was black and white again. So this is just one of the charming sights they treat us to, from time to time.

Feeding your seahorses

First thing in the morning your seahorses will all be waiting for their breakfast, and they will be dancing up and down begging for the food. If you are 5 minutes late you will be amazed at the looks on their little faces. Enough to make you feel so guilty.

If you try your seahorses on new food do expect them to be suspicious of it. It is best to introduce new food in the morning when they are most hungry, and do not forget to enrich the frozen food with vitamins once a week. There are many sorts on the market, just drip or spray the vitamins on the rinsed and drained frozen food and let it stand for a few minutes. The vitamins come in an oil base so that they stick to the food, but add them too often and you will clog up the pipes in your tanks.

So here they are ready and waiting for breakfast.

The same thing in the evening as you clean their tank ready for the night they will always try to get more food from you, but if you go just before lights out you will find most of them on their favourite hitches waiting for the night. For this reason I work the tank light with a timer so they get used to the same routine. While we have this photo just look at the top two seahorses, the black is the eyes of the unborn fry in the two males pouches. That is a sure indication that birthing is about to take place. Different species have larger or flatter pouches when about to give birth. My little H. Kuda look like they have swallowed marbles before they give birth.

Chapter 4

When the young seahorses are born

New born fry

I thought I would start this chapter off with this photo of a young seahorse that had just been

born.

See page 30 for young pregnant males seahorses. They are the ones with black pouches.

The new born seahorses (fry) are a perfect replica of mum and dad, and need to eat newly

hatched baby brine shrimp from birth. Instructions for hatching are further on in this chapter.

So your boy has had a very swollen womb and then the aquarium begins to fill with tiny seahorses. The first reaction is panic, but with good preparation this can be avoided. We are going to see all the things you can do to make this an exciting time for you, and hopefully, for you to raise your first fry. The name for baby seahorses.

Well before we talk about catching them, lets talk about safty for the fry, in the parent tank. If you have a weir then the fry can go straight through the grills to the sump below, or in the back of your tank. So each day, when you are expecting fry, cover the weir with a thin layer of filter wool, to catch the fry as they are released. My seahorses have their fry soon after the lights come on, but not always. They can arrive in the dark while you sleep or early morning or dinner time. I always say the males wait until I am just about to go out then they give me 200 fry.

Just a word of warning about covering the weir, make sure that the filter wool is thin enough to let the water through and do not let it clog up, as there is nothing worse than a flood to wake up to first thing in the morning.

If you have power heads then make sure they are covered where they take the water in and where they spout it out, as these can kill a lot of fry in a few seconds. Any other type of filter also needs covering. Popsocks work well as does filter wool, but make sure you rinse it every day. When the fry are born you can turn off the pumps and power heads, but do not forget to turn them back on, once you have caught the fry. This is important as the parent tank needs the water to be flowing all the time. Males flush their pouches at the time of the birthing so make sure the water is clean and a good water change is done a few days before hand. They flush a couple of days before giving birth to help the fry to adjust to the water they will be born into.

Catching the fry

This can be quite a challenge the first time, but a tiny cup or jug is useful, as all fry float to the top of the water at first. Using a turkey baster you can catch the ones that stay under the surface and if you have caught all the loose ones then you can take a jug , add some tank water and carefully drag the filter wool, with the fry on it, into the jug. Do it as quickly as you can and do not worry if they appear trapped in it. Left for half an hour in the jug (with an airline added) the majority can free themselves. Put more filter wool in place, as on the day of the birth the seahorses will release a few extra ones for most of that day.

The new tank for the fry to grow in.

I do prefer these tanks to any other for the fry for the first few weeks of their lives. I do not have a deal with the manufactures, it is just that they are so easy to manage for fry that can swim and hitch immediately. H. Erectus, H. Kuda and H. Barbouri come in this category and most other bethnic fry. (Fry that do not float for days once they are born). See photos on the next page.

The top of the tanks has a chamber where you can add some filter medium from your main tank filter, cover it with filter wool, and add some filter wool each side of the middle chamber. I also cover the end of the intake pipe with sponge. I cut a piece of filter sponge, bought in sheets for pond filters, to about 6 inches in height and 12 inches long, I wrap it around the intake pipe and hold it in place with elastic bands. Then I cover it with a pop sock. This eventually also becomes part of the filter, so rinse it in the used removed tank water, once a week.

Fry raising tanks

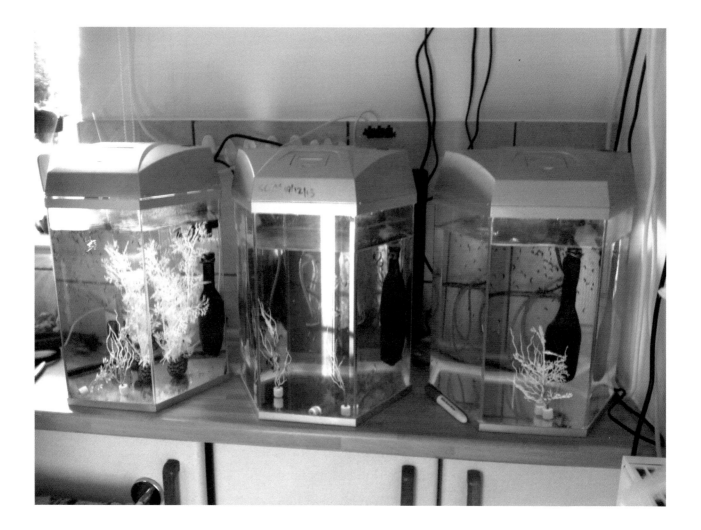

These are made by Den Marketing

The batch of seahorses can live in here for about three to four weeks then as the seahorses grow they have to be moved to a small grow out tank. I use ones that are about 40 litres and quite shallow so I can clear the food easily. Fry require a constant supply of baby brine shrimp, and I have 6 hatching vessels on the go to feed all mine plus rotifer and copepods. The rotifers are on the left and I feed them phytoplancton and take one litre out a day, even if no requirement for them, as they will have a population blow out and all die (the culture will crash).

Some of my rotifer and bbs hatching vessels

When the fry are growing they eat an amazing amount of live food, they eat and poo all day long. The greasy waste builds up a film on the bottom of the fry tanks and this has to be removed twice a day, and if you do not do this some of the fry will get caught by the mess and will die as it is also very toxic.

The fry tanks need to be checked for ammonia and nitrites every day and water changes done as required. This is so important as you will learn how much food to add and how much tank cleaning and water changing is required this way, with out killing the fry.

As the fry grow another source of rich fry food is copepods. I use the Tigriopus Californicus and raise them all the year round in buckets in the garden. They breed happily in any salinity and eat everything that falls in the buckets. Using a set of four sieves I can gather the pods and collect the waste quite quickly. The sieves separate the pods from the waste and are for sale on various sites as a set of hobby artimea sieves combi. They are also in a few pet shops, and are so useful in the growth of pods.

I have these tongue in cheek instructions for looking after my pods, which I send to people who want to start a culture.

These copepods are of mixed origin, coming from various buckets selected for their abundant activity. To keep them happy you should set their salinity at 1.024 and the natural resources will do the rest. Salinity must be between 0.00 and 0.35 or off the scale if it is hot. Gently drip

rainwater straight from the clouds for top up. Add salt water on occasion as you think necessary.

If the container were to overflow your pods would also wander off, so in stormy weather start

another bucket off by tipping some water from the full buckets into the empty one, this stops

them running off and helps to cultivate more pods. Always add phyto if the water is clear enough

to drink. These pods enjoy the hot sunlight and sleep well under 4 inches of ice in winter. They

love to munch on leaves, beetles, bees and other unfortunate beings that land in their buckets.

To spot the ones carrying egg sacks, they have two parts to their body, the others only have one.

In midwinter, if you need copepods, bring a bucket indoors and stand on newspaper

(condensation) and once the ice has defrosted give it a couple of days and the bucket will be

teaming with tiny copepods. Before letting them loose in your tank sieve some copepods, add to

clean salt water and add some phyto, leave for an hour then strain, rinse and feed to tank.

Chapter 5

Weaning the young seahorses

After a few weeks

The growing out and weaning of the fry is very tricky and is the time when we loose the most seahorses. The trick is to feed as much as they need without overloading the filtration. Lack of food and the water getting ammonia are two killers at this time.   I have large system tanks I use but the average seahorse keeper would likely do better with a stand alone tank similar to these. This one has a large surface space and I have added some filter media to the back, and I have covered the filter intake, using easily available plastic mesh (from a sieve sold in most supermarkets). I have put a smaller pump in so the flow does not pin the fry to the mesh where the water goes into the back of the tank. There are a lot of similar tanks on the market and they are very easy to start the weaning process off.

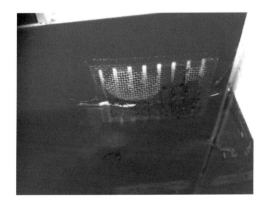

Close up of covered weir   Tank view, the weir is at the back

Each morning clean the tank bottom and feed the jouveniles on the following.

1   Baby brine newly hatched and copepods

2   Enriched artemia

3   Chopped mysis

Remove the chopped mysis after 1 hour as it can lay on the bottom and start to deteriorate, killing any fry sitting around it looking for a piece to eat. Repeat this for a week 3 times a day. Then drop off the baby brine shrimp, and after the second week give mysis first and then give the rest a few hours later. Drop off the enriched artimea once they are all taking the chopped mysis. You will soon be able to feed them whole small mysis and gradually they will grow and just need the mysis. Some will die during this process but if you make sure they are all eating all the time that will help reduce the deaths. Also keep the water in prime condition. These photos show the size to start weaning, and how they grow. These ones in the photo are 4 weeks old.

These are 8 weeks old and are on chopped mysis and copepods

At every stage it is important to keep the tank bottoms clean of waste and old uneaten food.

These are 12 weeks old and are on mysis now.

These can also have some copepods and live mysis now and then. They can be moved to a 130 litre tank to grow out in, but be careful that the weir is covered and any other water intakes in the tank. The power heads and filter boxes and any other water intake still needs covering until they get to about 4 inches, as they can get stuck against these and cannot feed, so very important to watch out for.

These are on mysis and are eating fine. They put on about half an inch a month at this age.

These are weaned and will soon be ready to sell.

At this age they love their mysis and can eat larger foods too. A mix of mysis and Mysis RS can

help them to grow and put on weight. They do love the occasional live mysis too, but be careful

not to undo all the weaning work you have already done. At this age they should never have

artimea (brine shrimp) as they will not get the goodness they need when they are growing up.

Chapter 6

Selling your seahorses

This is the sad part, and also exciting part. You have sucessfully raised your seahorses, you have probably kept some, and now you can not justify any more tanks in the house so you have to part with a few.

The thing I must mention here is the Pet Shop License. Everyone selling seahorses must have a license. They are easy enough to obtain from your local council, and then once you are properly registered with the authorities you can advertise your seahorses and sell them.

The Government would also be interested in any profits you make from a taxation point of view, so do keep good records.

You can advertise your seahorses as genuine aquarium bred seahorses and they will be highly desirable, as they will be free from disease and parasites.

When you sell them you should state that they are aquarium bred and their date of birth.

You could take some photos and approach the local fish shops, explaining that you are licensed and will sell them with an invoice and birth certificate.

You can not sell seahorses on eBay for two reasons

One is that they are a protected species and as such are closely monitored and need a CITES

certificate and because of being made aware of this eBay has stopped the selling of seahorses

live or dead on the UK site.

Two is they could be purchased by someone who has a totally unsuitable tank, and they could die

if not properly looked after, so it is not kind to the seahorse either.

When the seahorse is bred by yourselves, if you sell on eBay you would not be able to check that

the prospective purchaser has a suitable sized, fully cycled, marine tank to put them in. As a

responsible breeder you would have to make sure that the new owners understand how to keep

seahorses, as these are not the normal, run of the mill, marine fish. They are delicate and have

special requirements. This is done by asking polite questions and offering some information

about how to keep them.

You may find it useful to prepare a care sheet for the new owner telling them how you do it.

Stating the salinity, the temperature, the lighting period and times they get fed. The food you

use, even the salt you use, all this is of interest to the new owner.

When they come to pick their seahorses up make sure you have suitable polystyrene boxes and

heat pads to keep them warm and protected on their journey.   Strong bags are essential and only fill them with enough water to cover the seahorse and leave the rest of the bag for air. Buy bags large enough to take one third water and two thirds air. Always put some macro algae for hitches in the bag so the seahorses can hold onto the hitches and have a sleep on the way home. This will make their transition to their new home more comfortable. The less stressed they are on the journey the better they will settle when they get to their destination.

There is always a demand for these beautiful creatures so I wish you well with your selling them.

Chapter 7

When your seahorse is ill

Symptoms

Gas bubbles in the pouch

If your male seahorse is unable to swim properly and is floating , belly up some of the time, he likely has gas in his pouch. This can be cured very easily by releasing the gas from his pouch. Hold the seahorse with your finger and thumb on his body near the top of the pouch. Let him curl his tail around your little finger and once he has a grip he will relax. So with your thumb on the right hand, start massaging the gas up to the top of the pouch from the very bottom of the pouch. Be very gentle but firm enough to move the gas upwards. When it gets to the top of the pouch it may not come out of the womb. You may need to press slightly on the top end of the slot in the front of the womb with something sterile and not sharp.   You could clean a tiny round piece of plastic such as a price tag holder, and gently open the womb at the top while massaging the womb further down, towards the top. The gas will come out in the form of bubbles and may be accompanied by a popping sound. The seahorse will get immedite relief. The cause of this could be one of many things, but most common is a piece of dirt in the water getting into his womb when he flushed it. A dead fry left over from the last birthing or just the water quality of the tank being under par. Once you have released the gas do a large water change and he should return to normal.

White tip on the tail

This is usually caused by infection after getting the tail injured or after a temperature rise. When the temperature rises the bacteria in the tank increase. This can cause infection in the tail. You could try a large water change and cleaning the tail tip with a drop of iodine to a quantity of water. Say 50 ml water to 1 drip of tincture of iodine. Remove the seahorse from the tank in a 2 litre jug of water, and keeping his body and head below the water, just use some cotton wool with the iodine mixture on it to dab gently on his tail. This acts as a disinfectant and cleanses the area. This and the water change may be all that is necessary.

If the tail does not improve find an exotic vet near you and take the seahorse to the vet. It will need antibiotics. Transport the seahorse in a fish bag filled one third with water and the seahorse and a hitch, and two thirds with air. Put the bag into a polystyrene box and add something that will keep the seahorse warm. There are heatpacks, but it is unlikely you would have one, so a warm hot water bottle wrapped in a towel so that it is just taking the chill off will do. Better to keep the hot water bottle in the box separated by newspaper from the seahorse.

A seahorse can get injured by the heater if it is not covered as they hitch onto it. This would be a burn down the side of the seahorse. Again seek vetinary assistance with this. Avoidance is better than waiting for an accident to happen. Cover the heater.

Boils and ulcers

Seahorses sometimes exhibit boils on their body or tail. These are caused by injury such as their gripping onto a bristle worm, or internal infection.

If you can see bristle worm spines in their tail try to pull them out with tweesers, but keep the seahorse under water at all times. If it is an abcess do not be tempted to burst it, but go to the vet and get antibiotics. My own vet is very reasonable and it is well worth the visit. I have helped injured seahorses to gain full health with the help of my vet.

If you get the bristle worm spines out dab the seahorse with the iodine mixture (see white tip on the tail on page 48) and do a large wate change. The injury sometimes becomes infected so a visit to the vet may be necessary.

The other issues that need medication are snout rot (white tip on snout and not eating) and pop eye. A large water change can be enough to help the seahorse to recover from these, again a visit to the vet may be necessary for antibiotics.

Difficulty snicking

The last issue is when they can not snick properly, this is caused by several things, either something lodged in the snout or an injury to the trigger, or an infestation of parasites in the gills which has spread to the snout. You can treat parasites in the gills by giving a Formalyn dip to the seahorse.

The way to do this is to put 10 litres of clean salt water into a container with an airline, and add 2 ml of Formalyn per every 10 litres of water, turn up the bubbles to thoroughly mix the water and aerate it then turn the bubbles slightly down again, then put the seahorses in the dip for 30 to 45 minutes, until the parasites have all come out of their gills. If they thrash around in the water it is because the parasites are leaving them.

I would use a vet if you suspect something is stuck in the snout, or it is damaged, as they need to be able to eat all the time, or they quickly fade away.

Just as you have a vet for your cat or dog I would recommend you find one for your seahorses before they get ill, so you have someone to help you if need be. You will need an exotic vet, one that deals with lizards and fish. I would also recommend that you find a close neighbour or relative or friend that can feed your seahorses when you need it, if you go away or something crops up that stops you being there. If these things are in place before you need them it makes it a lot easier for you when something occurs. Lastly I do hope that you have found this book interesting and that it has helped you to get started on keeping your new seahorses.

After thoughts

Suitable companions for seahorses

This is not a comprehensive list, more of a guide line, but very small and slow fish are best added to your seahorse tank, mandarines and scooter blennys for eating the waste food, small file fish for clearing aiptasia, and perhaps one or two other small fish for other cleaning. Six line wrass eat flatworm and do not compete for the seahorses food.

Unsuitable for seahorses

Algae blennies are not suitable as they rasp the seahorses skin to remove algae, causing the stress and possible injury. Tangs, as they can injure seahorses, fast moving fish as they get the food first, large fish as they stress the seahorses. Crabs are not good as they can injure the seahorse with their claws. Clams can catch their tails when they close quickly, and any stinging corals such as Euphyllia, Catalaphyllia, Fire corals and lace corals, Anemones and Zonantharia can sting them.

Suitable corals

Alcyoniidae, soft corals which are suitable and come in many shapes and colours, Gorgonian and Leather corals

The principal is this … if it stings bites or catches do not put it with your seahorses.

Macro Algaes

Macro algaes are wonderful for seahorses and remove nitrogen, but do learn how to care for them and keep them trimmed as they can go asexual and polute the water if you neglect them. There are many to choose from and Caulerpa Prolifica, Caulerpa Serulata, Chaetomorpha, Dragons Breath, Botryocladia red grape algae, green grape algae, and many more.

Working and feeding your seahorses

As I am with my seahorses most of the day, I have no trouble feeding them 4 times a day. For those of you who go off to work each day, you can still keep seahorses, just feed them on a frozen food that has been gamma radiated in the morning just before you go to work, or non radiated food when you get up, and clear any left overs before you go to work. Then on return feed them as soon after you arrive home as possible and again before their lights go out. So say 8am, 6pm and 8pm. This seems to give them a routine they can adjust to, and helps them live healthy lives.

Another way would be feed early, leave with some live food in the tank such as mysis and feed frozen at 6pm to 8 pm. River shrimp can also be left in the tank. Just be careful that they do not get attached to the live food and stop eating the frozen as live food is not always available.

Printed in Great Britain
by Amazon